Ten Chickens

Dominie Press, Inc.

Ten little chickens,
one fine day,
left mother hen
and went out to play.

One little chicken
hid in a shoe.

Along came another one.
That made two.

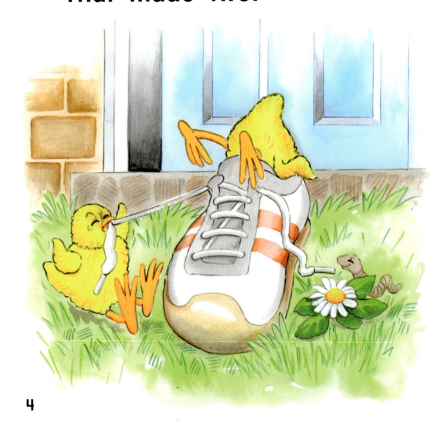

**Two little chickens
climbed up a tree.**

**Along came another one.
That made three.**

Three little chickens
sat on the floor.

Along came another one.
That made four.

**Four little chickens
learned how to dive.**

**Along came another one.
That made five.**

**Five little chickens
jumped over sticks.**

**Along came another one.
That made six.**

**Six little chickens
met a boy named Kevin.**

**Along came another one.
That made seven.**

Seven little chickens
ate off Kevin's plate.

Along came another one.
That made eight.

Eight little chickens danced in a line.

Along came another one. That made nine.

Nine little chickens
ran to mother hen.

Along came
the **last** one.
That made ten.

Ten little chickens,
cheep, cheep, cheep,
cuddled up, snuggled up,
and went to sleep.